The Really Wild Life of Snakes™

KING SNAKES

HEATHER FELDMAN

The Rosen Publishing Group's
PowerKids Press™
New York

For my precious Matthew Sam

Published in 2004 by The Rosen Publishing Group, Inc.
29 East 21st Street, New York, NY 10010

First Edition

Editor: Kathy Kuhtz Campbell
Book Design: Michael de Guzman, Mike Donnellan

Photo Credits: Cover, pp. 4, 4 (inset), 8 (inset), 11, 15, 20 © David A. Northcott/CORBIS; back cover, pp. 12, 16 (inset) © R. Andrew Odum/Peter Arnold, Inc.; pp. 7, 15 (inset), 19 © Carmela Leszczynski/Animals Animals; p. 8 © George H. H. Huey/Animals Animals; p. 16 © John Cancalosi/Peter Arnold, Inc.

Feldman, Heather.
King snakes / Heather Feldman.— 1st ed.
      p. cm.— (The really wild life of snakes)
Summary: Describes the physical characteristics, different species, and common behavior of king snakes.
Includes bibliographical references (p.   ).
ISBN 0-8239-6723-9 (library binding)
  1. Lampropeltis getulus—Juvenile literature. [1. King snakes. 2. Snakes.] I. Title. II. Series.
    QL666.O636 F447 2004
    597.96—dc21

                                                                                        2002015618

Manufactured in the United States of America

CONTENTS

VERY COMMON SNAKES

King snakes are nonpoisonous snakes that live in the United States and in southeastern Canada. Some king snakes live in Mexico and South America. Most of the king snakes you will learn about in this book live in the United States and are known as common king snakes. They have many similar features, but they vary in skin color and pattern. California king snakes are brown or black with white rings or yellow stripes on their bodies. Eastern king snakes are brown or black and have a yellow or white chainlike pattern. Speckled king snakes are black or brown with yellow spots on their scales. Black king snakes are all black.

Top: *King snakes, such as this speckled king snake, are members of the largest snake family, called Colubridae. Bottom: All king snakes, including this desert king snake, are related to milk snakes.*

KING SNAKE HOMES

King snakes live in many places. Black king snakes make their homes in the fields and woods of Ohio, Illinois, Georgia, and Alabama. California king snakes, desert king snakes, and Mexican black king snakes live in deserts and in brush in the Southwest and in California, Oregon, Utah, and Mexico. Eastern king snakes live in the forests, farmlands, and swamps of New Jersey and certain southern states, including Alabama. Florida king snakes live near **everglades**, streams, and canals in sugarcane fields in Florida. Speckled king snakes live near streams, forests, and farms in Louisiana, Mississippi, Arkansas, and Missouri.

King snakes, such as this eastern king snake, can grow to be from 3 to 7 feet (0.9–2.1 m) long. King snakes can be found hiding under logs, in woodpiles, or in piles of leaves.

RANGE OF COMMON KING SNAKES

COLD-BLOODED KINGS

King snakes are cold-blooded. Their body **temperature** is similar to the temperature that is around them. However, snakes need to keep their body temperature at a steady level. They adjust their body heat by changing their surroundings. If the sun's rays become too hot, king snakes must find cool shade or they will die from too much heat. During very cold weather, they need to find shelter to stay alive. Most snakes **hibernate** during winter. They dig into the ground or find dens and sleep all winter. Come spring, a king snake will slither out of its den, warm itself in the sun, and begin hunting again.

Mexican black king snakes and desert king snakes, such as the ones seen here, live in deserts. Desert snakes hibernate during very hot, dry periods, unlike snakes that hibernate during cold periods.

THE KING OF ALL SNAKES

King snakes are **constrictors**. They wrap their bodies around their **prey** and squeeze it until the prey **suffocates**. They can kill small animals, such as mice, in a few minutes. Larger prey, such as a lizard, might take several hours to kill. They also eat other snakes. They can even eat poisonous snakes, including rattlesnakes and coral snakes. The **venom** from these snakes usually does not harm a king snake. That is why it is called the king of all snakes. Its favorite meals are **rodents**, frogs, and birds. King snakes swallow their prey whole and headfirst. They are often **diurnal**, but can be **nocturnal** in hot weather.

This California king snake is eating a rattlesnake. King snakes also eat fish, frogs, birds, mice, and lizards. After eating big prey, a king snake might not eat again for four months.

SNAKEBITE
LAMPROPELTIS GETULUS IS THE SCIENTIFIC NAME FOR KING SNAKES. *LAMPROPELTIS*, A LATIN WORD, MEANS "SHINY SHIELDS" IN ENGLISH.

SEEKING A MATE

After hibernation, king snakes look for **mates**. Female king snakes produce a scent to attract male king snakes. This scent tells the male king snakes when the females are ready to mate, which is usually between March and June. Sometimes two male snakes will fight over the same female king snake. The male snakes perform a **combat** dance. First one snake tries to get past the other. Then they wrap their bodies around each other and lift up their heads and the top part of their bodies. The stronger snake pins the other one down. The weaker snake slithers away. The winner mates with the female.

◄ *Male and female king snakes mate in the spring. When she is ready to mate, a female king snake gives off a scent that draws a male to her.*

KING SNAKE BABIES

Female king snakes usually lay their cream-colored eggs from May to August. Female king snakes can lay between 3 and 24 oval-shaped eggs at one time. This group of eggs is called a **clutch**. The eggs hatch between 8 ½ and 11 ½ weeks later, mostly in late summer. King snake babies are usually from 8 to 12 inches (20–30.5 cm) long when they hatch. They are a darker color than their parents are. This dark color hides them from **predators**. As soon as they hatch, they must find food and shelter on their own. Baby king snakes like to eat insects, worms, and baby mice. As they grow, their colors brighten. Baby king snakes become adults in about two to four years.

Top: An eastern king snake is laying her eggs. Bottom: The colors of most king snakes lighten as they grow older. The colors of this young Florida king snake could become even brighter as it ages.

SPECIAL FEATURES

A king snake's backbone has from 100 to 400 small bones called **vertebrae**. Except for those in the neck and the tail, each vertebra is connected to a pair of separate, thin ribs. This structure, or frame, allows a king snake to coil, to climb, and to move in S curves across the ground. A king snake also has a **hinged** jaw. The jaw can stretch. The bones in the upper jaw and in the lower jaw can move separately from one another. They can even stretch sideways. This hinged jaw allows a snake to open its mouth wide to swallow prey that can be several times bigger than its head. The sharp, curved teeth help the snake to hold prey and to move it down the throat.

Top: *Having a lot of vertebrae allows this speckled king snake to bend easily.* Bottom: *The hinged jaw of this king snake enables it to open its mouth wider than its head to swallow a rattlesnake.*

GETTING RID OF ENEMIES

King snakes are usually calm and gentle snakes. However, when a king snake believes that it is in danger it will try to protect itself in several ways. The king snake **vibrates** its tail. The sound of the tail as it moves quickly back and forth against leaves or the ground scares predators away. The king snake also hisses and tries to bite its enemies. If it is attacked, a king snake rolls itself up, keeping its head in the center. Then it sprays the enemy with a bad-smelling **substance**, called musk, and body wastes. Some of the king snake's enemies include skunks, opossums, raccoons, owls, and hawks.

To defend itself, sometimes a king snake, such as this speckled king snake, will roll itself up. It will also rattle its tail, spray musk, and release body wastes to frighten predators.

SNAKEBITE
ALL SNAKES MOLT, OR SHED THEIR OLD OUTER LAYER OF SKIN, WHEN A NEW LAYER HAS GROWN UNDER THE OLD ONE.

SNAKE SENSES

A king snake cannot hear or see as well as people can. Its eyes are on the sides of its head, which makes it hard for the snake to see far away. It relies on its senses of taste and smell to find prey. Its forked tongue flicks in and out of the mouth. As the tongue goes back into the mouth, the snake's **Jacobson's organ** helps to taste and to smell scents.

A king snake does not have eardrums. To hear, it uses its jawbones to feel vibrations in the ground. The vibrations are carried to its inner ear by bones in the snake's head. From the vibrations a king snake can tell if its prey is approaching or is running away.

A king snake's fork-shaped tongue and its Jacobson's organ, which is located in the roof of the mouth, allow the snake to smell and taste its surroundings. King snakes have an excellent sense of smell.

HOW KING SNAKES HELP PEOPLE

King snakes are harmless snakes to people. They are often very helpful. King snakes help farmers by eating rats and mice. These rodents can carry illnesses to farm animals and can eat crops. By eating these pests, the snakes help to stop the spread of sicknesses.

Many people like to keep king snakes as pets. They believe that king snakes are very tame, are easy to care for, and are fun to watch. However, some people believe that king snakes are happiest in their own natural **habitats**. Whether in a person's home or in a snake's natural habitat, a king snake is an interesting creature to admire and to study.

22

GLOSSARY

clutch (KLUCH) The number of eggs laid by a female snake at one time.

combat (KOM-bat) A battle or a fight.

constrictors (kun-STRIKT-urz) Snakes that kill by wrapping their bodies around their prey and squeezing.

diurnal (dy-UR-nul) Active during the daytime.

everglades (EH-ver-glaydz) Areas of swampy, low ground with thick grasses.

habitats (HA-bih-tats) The surroundings where animals or plants naturally live.

hibernate (HY-bur-nayt) To spend the winter in a sleeplike state.

hinged (HINJD) Attached by a joint that moves back and forth or up and down. King snakes have hinged jaws that allow them to swallow animals that are bigger than their own heads.

Jacobson's organ (JAY-kub-sunz OR-gun) A kind of sensory organ that helps snakes' senses of taste and smell. It is located in the roof of a snake's mouth.

mates (MAYTS) Male and female animals that come together to make babies.

nocturnal (nok-TUR-nul) Active during the night.

predators (PREH-duh-terz) Animals that kill other animals for food.

prey (PRAY) An animal that is hunted by another animal for food.

rodents (ROH-dents) Animals with gnawing teeth, such as mice.

substance (SUB-stans) Matter that takes up space.

suffocates (SUH-fuh-kayts) Dies from lack of air.

temperature (TEM-pruh-cher) The heat in a living body.

venom (VEH-num) A poison passed by one animal into another through a bite or a sting.

vertebrae (VER-tuh-bray) Backbones, which protect the spinal cord. A king snake can have from 100 to 400 vertebrae in its backbone.

vibrates (VY-brayts) Moves back and forth quickly.

INDEX

WEB SITES

Due to the changing nature of Internet links, PowerKids Press has developed an online list of Web sites related to the subject of this book. This site is updated regularly. Please use this link to access the list:
www.powerkidslinks.com/rwls/king/

24